THE LITTLE BOOK OF RESILIENCE

Joe & Melody Cheal

Published in England
by GWiz Publishing
Oakhurst, Mardens Hill,
Crowborough, E. Sussex.
TN6 1XL

Tel (+44) 1892 309205

First published 2018
10 9 8 7 6 5 4 3

© Joe & Melody Cheal 2018

Illustrations by Rob Banbury
All illustrations © 2018

All rights reserved.
No part of this publication may be reproduced, in any way, without prior permission of the authors.

ISBN: 978-0-9955979-2-1

CONTENTS

Bouncing Back   1

In the Driving Seat   31

The Way You See It   59

Meaning, Purpose & Wellbeing 83

Change How You Feel   111

About Us   133

ACKNOWLEDGEMENTS

To the thousands of people who have added to this book with their ideas and questions in coaching and training sessions.

INTRODUCTION

For over 25 years, we have been fascinated by what makes people 'psychologically strong and healthy'.

Following that curiosity, we have observed, listened to, read about and engaged with some very 'sorted' human beings.

By modelling the behaviours, qualities, characteristics and thought processes of many of these wonderful human beings, we have developed a range of ideas, models, tools, tips and techniques to help others remain strong when life and work gets tough.

HOW TO USE THIS BOOK

The Little Book of Resilience is a 'dip in' book, designed to give you an idea on each page that you might reflect on and wherever possible, take action.

For each idea, consider:

Where do I do that already?
Where could I do that more often?
Where could I begin doing that?
How might I do that?
With whom?

BOUNCING BACK!

BOUNCING BACK!

THE BOUNCE BACK FACTOR?

Think back to times in the past when you have 'bounced-back'.
How long did it take?

Most likely, it depends on the situation.
Sometimes it takes time to bounce back.

There are moments in life where it might seem odd if we bounced back and recovered immediately.

Psychologically healthy people know that bouncing back is a process we go through (and hence out the other side). Sometimes it happens quickly and sometimes it takes a little longer.

PSYCHOLOGICAL FITNESS AND TOUGHNESS

Presumably, you wouldn't go to the gym once and then declare yourself fit for life!

Resilience is like a form of fitness. It is important to stay with the programme! Make sure you continue to develop new strategies, whilst reminding yourself of the tools that really work for you. Take time to reflect and learn.

We all need a bit of maintenance!

Resilient people make a choice to stay mentally, emotionally and (of course) physically fit.

TRANSFORM!

For many people, the desire and ability to become more psychologically healthy comes from a transformational moment... perhaps a revelation or a significant realisation.

Whilst sometimes we reach these transformational moments alone, more often they happen when we are with others, perhaps on a personal development course, or with a coach or having honest and open discussions with our partner or with friends.

Where do you seek support?

Resilient people understand that transformation happens when we are ready for it... and so they aim to stay in a permanent state of 'open to change'!

MAKE A RESILIENT DECISION

Are you aware that because
resilience is a state of mind,
it is simply a choice!

When do you choose to be resilient?

Go on… decide to be resilient… now!

*When we decide to be resilient, the brain
begins to filter our experiences differently.*

YOU ARE BRILLIANT!

It is a remarkable moment when you realise that you don't need to do anything to <u>be</u> brilliant!

Did you know that
you are enough and that *you have value and worth as a human being.*

Resilience is connected to strong self-esteem and positive self-regard.

MODEL THE BEST!

Think about the most resilient people you know. Write a list of qualities and characteristics that they have.

Who do you know that you would consider 'Resilient'?
What is it about them?
How do they think?
How do they handle pressure?

*Resilient people are worth modelling.
They can teach us a lot!*

MODEL... YOURSELF!

Have you noticed that there are certain contexts where you are more resilient than others?

Notice the difference... how do you approach and handle the situation when you are resilient?

How might you transfer those skills, qualities and resources to situations where you want to be stronger?

*Resilience is inside all of us.
All we have to do is 'map it across' to situations where we might be less confident.*

LOTS OF STRATEGIES!

Consider a high-pressure situation (e.g. you are delivering an important presentation and someone asks a question that you don't know the answer to!)

How many different approaches do you have for dealing with that?

Resilient people tend to have a range of strategies for dealing with situations. Only having one approach is a risk… what happens if it doesn't work!

MORE THAN ONE WAY TO BOUNCE BACK!

Use the ideas from this book to write down at least 10 different techniques you can use to bounce back and feel good again!

Make sure you have a range of 'recoveries', so that if one method doesn't help you get back on your feet, another one will.

ALLOW YOURSELF TIME TO RECOVER

If you are finding it hard to bounce back, acknowledge that there may be a healing process that will take a bit of time.

What is your process?
What stages do you go through as part of your healing process?

Sometimes life throws massive curveballs and googlies!
In these cases, we need time to recover –
there might not be an instant fix.

BABY STEPS!

When you face an apparent mountain, ask yourself: "What's the next smallest step I can take to help me in the direction I want to go?"

When we take a tumble, it may take a bit of determination and tenacity to get back up and carry on.
Consider the motivation of a small child learning to walk. They fall down, get back up and give it another go.
Be inspired by the baby steps of a small child…

RUN YOUR OWN BRAIN!

Get curious as to how you think about the world out there… about yourself… about other people… about your job and the place you work…
If you have some negative thoughts, bring them to the surface by writing them down… then consider how they affect you.

The most resilient people tend to own their experience of the world -
they understand that the way they think about the world will affect the quality of their life.
If you are not running your brain, who is?

BEATINGS ARE NOT COMPULSORY!

If you ever realise that you are beating yourself up about something, STOP! Then reflect on what happened, think of other ways you might have handled it… then move on!

When things go wrong, you have a set of choices. Some people beat themselves up (perhaps they know no other way). Resilient people rarely give themselves a hard time (unless it is part of their motivation strategy)… they reflect, they learn and they move on.

IT'S ALL A BIT OF A LAUGH!

Have you ever said to yourself:
"One day I'll probably
look back at this and laugh"?
If so, why wait!
If you were a comedian, how would
you tell this story now?

*The ability to laugh is a gift in
the face of adversity.
Resilience can often be a case of seeing the
silly side of a situation.
Sometimes troubling situations are
absurd… so treat them as such.*

DEVELOP MENTAL FITNESS

Consider resilience and wellbeing as something to maintain… by keeping a journal of the things that work for you, you will develop lots of tools and techniques to keep you mentally healthy and happy.
Find out more about the human potential movement and positive psychology.
Read some quality 'self-help' books.

Resilience and wellbeing are our natural state of being. However, we may also have a set of unhelpful beliefs and reactions that throw us into anxiety, stress and panic. To bring ourselves back to our natural state and to hold ourselves there takes 'mental fitness'… something we need to develop and return to in order to stay strong.

ALLOW YOURSELF TIME TO RECOVER

Discover more about yourself and be open to transformational change.
Attend and fully participate in reputable personal development courses.
Seek out extraordinary counsellors, coaches and mentors.

Another way to manage our levels of resilience is to create shifts in our limiting beliefs and reactions.
This takes a significant change, something 'transformational' at the level of our self-esteem.
Remember however, that transformation rarely happens on your own.

MAKE TIME FOR OTHERS

Develop a network of people you connect with. It doesn't matter if you see people one-to-one or in groups… when you have a connection, give that person some of your time and be prepared to share something of yourself with them.

Resilient people engage with other people. They are not necessarily extroverts, they simply understand the importance of connection, company, companionship and friendship.
They do not isolate themselves, they are there for others that need help and they reach out for others when they need help themselves.

LIFE IS LEARNING

Whatever happens in life, ask yourself: "What constructive things can I learn from this?"

Life is a playground and the more we learn, the more we can grow and develop as human beings.

Resilient people learn from their experiences and update the way they perceive the world accordingly. They treat each experience as an opportunity to become wiser!

LEARN FOR THE FUTURE

When things don't go the way you expect (or want) them to,
rather than dwelling on what went wrong, ask yourself:

What could I do differently next time?

The act of focussing on the future helps you make changes in your life.
Dwelling on the past changes nothing… it has already happened!

Resilient people aim to improve themselves and to do no harm. They also understand that to say or do the 'wrong thing' is part of being human.
For that reason, they learn, forgive and move on.

SEEK OPPORTUNITIES

Wherever you are and whatever happens to you, try asking yourself:

What is good about this?
Where/when might this be
a good thing?
What are the opportunities here?

Resilience is often about seeing the possibilities in a situation.
This is why resilient people often seem so creative, flexible and successful.

DON'T 'CAN'T'!

Here's a simple one…

If you ever hear yourself say:
"I'm no good at this (or that)" or
"I can't do this (or that)",
remember that this is a <u>lie</u>!

Change what you say to:
"I could learn how to do this (or that)"
or "I could certainly improve my
ability to do this (or that)"

Confidence comes from believing in ourselves. The way we do that is to stop limiting ourselves and accept instead that we can learn to do things if we practice. Of course, there may be physical constraints, but resilient people understand the difference between physical and psychological limits.

LEARN TO ACHIEVE

As a way of removing excuses for not getting what we want in life, consider:

Whatever you want to achieve in life, there is probably somebody somewhere in the world (or in history) who started with less resources than you and who achieved what you want to achieve… and more!

Those who refuse to limit themselves often find inspiration in other people.

LEARN FROM FEEDBACK (1)

Feedback can come from the results we get, and it can come from other people…

Choose to welcome feedback, even when it is not delivered well!
Acknowledge both criticism and praise with grace…
Ask for more information (or for examples) if it helps you to get clear,
De-personalise it for a moment and consider the wider context / bigger picture.

Resilient people welcome feedback as it may be an opportunity to learn and develop.

LEARN FROM FEEDBACK (2)

Just because someone gives you feedback, criticism or praise… doesn't mean it is the Truth!

It is simply someone else's perspective.

Even if you don't agree with a generalised criticism, take time to evaluate the data and then self-review.

Resilience can mean treating feedback as data. Not only is it useful to gather data from others (and evaluate it), it may also give you clues about the person who gave you the feedback… i.e. how they perceive the world, what they believe to be right and what is important to them.
This can also be useful data!

ACCEPT THE PRAISE!

If someone gives you praise and you automatically reject or deflect it…
STOP!
Instead, say: "thank-you"!

Even though this is someone else's perspective, they cared enough to tell you.

Take a moment to evaluate the praise properly. Allow yourself to be open to accept it.

Resilient people accept positive feedback as easily as they accept any other type of feedback.

HANDLING MISTAKES

If you have made a mistake, the strongest and most courageous thing you can do is admit it and where necessary, let others know.
It is okay to make mistakes!

Paradoxically, you can add to your credibility by admitting a mistake… because people tend to find you more integrous, truthful and honest.

Resilient people tend to treat mistakes as a learning point… then they seek to make better decisions in the future.

IT'S OKAY NOT TO KNOW <u>EVERYTHING</u>!

If someone asks you a question and you don't know the answer, say so.

Just because you don't know the answer, does not make you a lesser person.

Where appropriate you can seek to find the answer and come back to them.

Resilient people know that knowledge and self-worth are different things.

BOUNCING BACK!

IN THE DRIVING SEAT

IN THE DRIVING SEAT

GET IN THE DRIVING SEAT

Too many people sit in the passenger
seat of their own life,
waiting for someone else to drive.
Some then complain that their life is
not what they want it to be!

Use this book to
take control of your life!

*Resilience involves getting out of the
passenger seat and driving one's own
experience.*

OWN YOUR STUFF!

The first step to getting in the driving seat is owning your own part in your experience. Whatever happens in life, you have choices.

Recognise that you are more in control of your experience than may at first be apparent.

Learn to recognise that you are responsible for how you respond to events that happen to you. Instead of blaming yourself or others start taking back your power.

Resilience means owning your stuff!

NOTICE THE PATTERNS (1)

By taking self-ownership you start to recognise patterns in relationships. This is the first step to an understanding of where these patterns began and with whom.

If you have a difficult interaction with someone, ask yourself:
How else could I see the situation?
What else might have caused this?
What could I do differently in future?

*Resilience means having
a flexible mind-set.
The ability to shift our mind-set allows us
to take a step back from situations and
consider what is really going on.*

NOTICE THE PATTERNS (2)

You <u>can</u> control how you interact with the world but you cannot <u>make</u> anyone else change.

However, if you change what you are doing, thinking, feeling and behaving it will usually create changes in the world around you!

Resilient people take ownership of their experience. This helps them to become more resourceful and more connected with their authentic self.

COMPLETING THE JIGSAW PUZZLE

Consider yourself like
a jigsaw-puzzle piece.

Notice how you interlock with others.

Where necessary, allow yourself
to 're-shape' your part of
any unhelpful puzzles.
Create a new jigsaw that is better
for all involved!

Resilience is about being flexible enough to avoid getting locked into 'dramas' with other people.

CHANGING THE SCRIPT

Sometimes we are so attached
to being right we forget that
we'd rather be happy!

These are often two opposing 'scripts'.

Make the decision now:
do you want to be right or
do you want to be happy?

Happiness is a choice.
You can choose to make changes in yourself
and your scripts…
that will give you a happier life!

LEARNING ABOUT YOURSELF

Take the time to learn more about yourself by studying fields of thought like: Positive Psychology,
Social Psychology,
Transactional Analysis,
Neuro-linguistic programming (NLP),
Wellbeing and
Body-Mind-Spirit.

By understanding what makes you tick, you can then form strategies that will allow you to respond more positively to other people and to life in general.

Resilient people seek to learn more about the human condition… particularly those linked with positivity, resilience and human potential.

CHANGE YOUR OWN BEHAVIOUR

It is pointless seeking happiness by asking someone else to change! Instead, you need to take ownership and make your changes first.

To do this ask yourself the following question: "What is it that I can do differently to change the situation?"

Resilient people understand that happiness comes from within. Whilst happiness may be influenced by external experiences, it is not *dependant on others.*

BRING IT BACK TO WHAT YOU <u>CAN</u> DO (1)

Decide what you <u>can</u> do
something about and
take action to make things better.

Ask yourself: What is within my
control and influence?

*The most resilient people tend to focus on
what they **can** do something about.*

BRING IT BACK TO WHAT YOU <u>CAN</u> DO (2)

If you are faced with a problem that is outside your control or influence, ask yourself: "How does that affect me directly?"
Whatever the answer, focus on solving the problem here: "And what can I do about how it affects me?"

Some issues are simply outside of our control. We cannot do anything about them. However, in order to be a problem for us, an issue must still impact on us in some way.
The trick here is to focus on how the issue impacts on you and then deal with the impact.

HANDLING A LACK OF DIRECTION

If you need to get something done but are not getting direction from others:

First, do some research and reflect. Then, from what you know, decide the best way forward.

Second, communicate (to the relevant others) what action you are going to take. They will soon tell you if they want you to do something different.

Third, take action!

To be resilient is to be proactive. A lack of direction from others does not mean we cannot act.

TAKE TIME TO PONDER

Think before acting. Take control of the way you 'bounce back'.
If you are in a situation that you find challenging, how do you sometimes react?
Now <u>think</u>… how might you do things differently in the future?

Consider the difference between reacting and responding…
To react is to 'reactivate' without control.
To respond implies a thinking process between a stimulus and how you handle it.

DRIVE YOUR FUTURE

Take time occasionally to predict and prepare for the future!
How might things be in
5-10 years' time?
If what you predict comes to pass, how will your job/environment be different?
How would/could your life be?
How will you be ready to handle and make the best of that future?

Resilient people keep a view beyond the present. They like to see how the threads of the past might weave into possible futures. For each future they imagine…
they have a plan.

HANDLING AN UNCERTAIN FUTURE

If you are unsure which path the future will follow, start by writing down the possible paths that could happen.
Then for each path, fill in the following:
If X happens, then I will…
If Y happens, then I will…
If Z happens, then I will…

Resilient people have contingency plans for the future. This helps them to feel in control and gives them more happiness and security.
Even if something else happens (outside their predictions), they seem better able to adapt their plans to handle what arises.

WHAT CAN YOU CHANGE?

If you are in a situation you don't like, consider the following ways you might approach that situation.

How might you:
- Change the situation?
- Change your location?
- Change your behaviour?
- Change how you see it?
- Change how you feel about it?

Also, what would happen if you did nothing?

There will always be options.
The trick is to figure out what they are!

TAKE CONTROL OF YOUR ENVIRONMENT

If you want to get organised but find that your environment is getting messy and cluttered… stop and tidy up. Put things away!

Alternatively, if you want to get creative, a messy environment may be just the thing!

A tidier environment can help us to feel more organised and in control. However, research suggests that a messy environment can be conducive to creative thinking. Resilient people tend to choose the best environment to help them achieve what they want!

DRIVE YOUR OUTCOME

Rather than moan about what's wrong, focus instead on what you want and where you want to get to.
Ask yourself:
- What is my outcome here?
  - What do I need?
  - What do I want?
- How do I want to feel differently?

When the going gets tough, the mentally tough get going, by focussing on their outcome… i.e. what they want to make happen and where they want to get to.

POSITIVE FOCUS

Make sure you focus on <u>what you want</u> (and/or what you want to have happen), rather than what you don't want.

A negative goal (i.e. what you don't want) tends to take a person in the direction of the very thing they are trying to get away from!

OWN IT!

Take responsibility for what you want to achieve. Make sure that your focus is about <u>your role</u> in achieving your goals.

Communicate with others and ask them for help by all means, but don't make them responsible for you achieving your goals in life.

Goals about other people doing things tend to be problematic.
We cannot <u>make</u> anybody do anything!

UNDERSTAND YOUR UNDERLYING DRIVERS

Get clear about <u>why</u> you want what you want.

If you were to get what you want, ask yourself:
What will that give me?
How will it benefit me?
What would I get by having it?

There will usually be more than one way to satisfy your underlying drivers/motives.

By understanding the underlying drivers for getting what we want, this will give us more flexibility in meeting those needs and desires.

MAKE IT MEASURABLE

Take time to get a sense of where you are and what you have achieved so far. Ask yourself the question: "How will I know I have achieved my goals?"
This will give you a way of gauging how you are doing...
and when you are done!

Resilient people have measures in place to make sure they are on track and also to determine when it is time to tick the 'achieved' box and move on.

DETERMINATION!

Set a deadline to anything you want to make happen.
This will help you to focus on what matters and motivate you in making sure you achieve your goals.

Resilient people are determined.
And they do this by making sure that their goals are determined too!
This is what helps them bounce back and get focussed again.

IT'S OKAY TO ASK FOR HELP

It is okay to ask for help
when you need it!

If you need help, be clear about what
help you need.

And remember that your self-worth
is not reliant on whether
they say yes or no!

Other people have the right to say 'no'
and this has nothing to do with who
you are as a person!

*Resilience can mean knowing when we are
at the edge of our knowledge or resources…
and being prepared to request help.*

IT'S OKAY TO ASK FOR WHAT YOU WANT

In any given situation, get specific about what you want or need.

Be clear in your communication.
Do not expect others to mind-read!

Recognise though, that asking does not equate to entitlement. People have the right to refuse or not respond…
so have a back-up plan!

*If people don't ask for what they want…
they usually don't get it!*

IT'S OKAY TO SAY 'NO'

Other people may sometimes want
things from you… for example:
your time, your attention, your money,
your affection, your space,
your belongings…

It is your choice to maintain your
boundaries and say 'no' or
'not at the moment'.
(If you find it hard to say 'no' to a
person, try imagining them in your
mind and then saying no to them!)

Of course, if you say 'no' to a
reasonable request (especially if you
are being paid to do a job)… be ready
to handle the consequences!

*Resilient people are more confident at
refusing requests but they are also prepared
to take and handle the consequences!*

IN THE DRIVING SEAT

**THE WAY
YOU SEE IT**

THE WAY YOU SEE IT

PERCEPTION IS REALITY!

You have a unique way of perceiving the world based on your personal filters.

When you experience a problem or find yourself in conflict with others, practice asking yourself: "what could be a different perception of this situation?"

Filters are developed during our early experiences.
Other people will have their own unique filters operating too.
When we take our filters literally, the 'illusion of reality' is often mistaken for truth!

THE GROWTH MINDSET

To further your 'growth mind-set', take a step back when things go wrong…

Look at the bigger picture…

What skills could you learn to better handle situations like this in the future?

A 'growth mind-set' is an overarching belief that we <u>can</u> develop ourselves and our abilities.
By believing this, we are more likely to put time and effort into self-improvement.

WHAT ABOUT LUCK?

No matter whether you believe
you are lucky or unlucky…

Write down a list of how and where in
your life you <u>are </u>(and <u>have been</u>) lucky.

*Research suggests that the difference
between lucky people and unlucky people is
simply <u>perception</u>.
Lucky people tend to be much happier…
and happy people tend to see themselves
as luckier!*

RESEARCH YOUR OWN LUCK

How do you review
your life experiences?

Notice what happens when you switch
your focus to the <u>positive</u> aspects of an
upsetting experience.

Although the event cannot be changed
you <u>can</u> change how you process
the experience.

*Different people could have
a similar experience…
but how they process that experience will
then determine how they feel about it.*

NOTICING OPPORTUNITIES (1)

How open are you to opportunities?

To become a luckier person, change your focus to the big picture.
Ask yourself: "What else is going on around me here?"

Research demonstrates that lucky people get more opportunities simply because they notice the opportunities when they arise!

NOTICING OPPORTUNITIES (2)

As well as being open-minded psychologically, you can also do this with your sight…

Focus on something in your surroundings… then 'soften' and broaden your gaze so you notice all the things around it… then soften more and notice all the other things in your field of vision.

'Softening' or broadening our field of sight is known as 'peripheral vision'…
and this can help to engender a calmer and more relaxed state of mind.

ADJUST YOUR 'LOCUS OF CONTROL'

When things happen that trouble you, start by checking how much control you perceive you have over the situation.

Take a deep breath and then ask yourself:
"What else do I have control over?"

As you identify other things within your control you will notice a sense of empowerment and choice.

'Locus of control' is the belief we have about how much control we have in life. The more control and fluidity a person develops in their <u>perception</u>, the more resilient they become.

GLASSES OF WATER!

Consider the metaphor about seeing a
glass as half-full or half-empty…
How do you perceive it…
optimistically or pessimistically?

The interpretation is your choice!

*Optimists tend to be more resilient
than pessimists.
However, 'realist optimists' may be even
more resilient!*

*In reality, the glass is always full!
It is half filled with water and
half filled with oxygen.
(And these are two essentials
we all need to survive!)*

THE VALUE OF OPTIMISM

When you adopt an optimistic mindset, you are setting yourself up for a generalised sense of improvement in your health and well-being.

To develop an optimistic mindset, focus on, notice, talk about and write down where you expect to experience the good things in life.

Optimists have a generalised sense of confidence about the future.

THE VALUE OF PESSIMISM

Does pessimism have a value?
Yes, it does! It is a primal survival mechanism developed to watch out for predators and other dangers.

In modern living you need it for risk assessments, contingency planning and checking your decisions.

When organising or deciding something, ask yourself:
"Is there any reason not to do this?"
"What could go wrong and how will I handle that?"

Resilient people learn to <u>live</u> in optimism but are able to step into pessimism when necessary.

BENEFITS OF BEING AN OPTIMIST

A simple exercise to develop
a more optimistic mindset
involves writing down (every day)
five positive experiences or
things/people you are grateful for.

Optimists experience less distress when dealing with difficulties in their lives. They adapt better to negative events and are capable of learning lessons from these experiences. Optimism predicts psychological and physical well-being. Optimists exert more continuous effort and are persistent when faced with challenges.

IT IS WHAT IT IS!

Sometimes, the most philosophical way to handle reality is to remind yourself: "It is what it is!"

Resilient people accept reality rather than denying it. They then make decisions as to what they want or need to do about it!

CLOSE THE FANTASY-REALITY GAP

If you find yourself *wishing* for something or believing that things *should* or *ought to* be different, then you are suffering from a 'fantasy-reality' gap.
Unmet expectations equal disappointments!
Close the gap by accepting the way things are... or be prepared to make changes in the world!

Resilience entails living in reality rather than pretending the world should fit your personal fantasy!

MANAGE YOUR EXPECTATIONS

Stop expecting the world to be different from what it is.

No amount of 'should' will fix it!

And stop waiting for other people to change who they are.

'If only' changes nothing!

*Resilient people seek to 'get real'
about the way the world is…
and they don't waste time wishing other
people were different.*

HAS IT GOT TO BE PERFECT?

A song may tell you that:
"It's got to be perfect…"
but perfection is often a fantasy.

If you are a perfectionist,
get used to saying the words:
"Good enough!"

Get fascinated by
the nature of imperfection…
and the imperfection of nature!

*Resilience is often about letting go of
the need for perfection!
Resilience means understanding
'good enough'.*

ENGAGE THE C.I.A.

If your reality isn't what you want it
to be… try the C.I.A.:
Change what you can change,
Influence what you can influence,
Adapt your perspective
to accept all the rest!

*Reinhold Niebuhr's 'Serenity Prayer'
says it beautifully:
"Grant me the serenity to accept the
things I cannot change,
courage to change the things I can,
and wisdom to know the difference."*

IF WE CAN'T CHANGE IT…

We can't always change the situation,
but we can change
how we see it,
how we feel about it and
how we react to it.

*Change your perception…
change your experience!*

SHIFTING PERSPECTIVE

Sometimes a set-back can seem bigger
than it really is.
You can put things
'back in perspective'
by asking questions like:

What's the worst that could happen?
Will this matter in 10 years' time?
In the scheme of things,
how big is this really?

*The art of resilience is often simply
the art of perspective.*

PROBLEM? WHAT PROBLEM?

Consider:
A problem is only a problem
if it is perceived as a problem!
A problem is not in the thing itself but
in the meaning we give it.

*Resilient people treat the things
that happen to (and around) them
as 'events' and 'situations'.
Then they take action
to improve matters!*

DEALING WITH PROBLEMS (1)

If you feel like you have a problem,
ask yourself two questions:

How is that a problem really?

How is that <u>not</u> a problem?

Notice where these questions take you.

*Resilient people ask themselves questions to
get the best perspective they can.*

DEALING WITH PROBLEMS (2)

Have you ever noticed how other people's problems are often easier to solve that your own?

To give yourself another perspective on a problem, ask yourself:

"If this was someone else's problem, what would I recommend?"

Resilience means becoming ever more resourceful and developing multiple ways of handling what life throws at us.

TAKING CRITICISM

If someone criticises you or perhaps accuses you of doing something that you didn't do… rather than get defensive, ask for more information!

Only then can we understand where the other person is coming from and what they believe to be true.

By gaining more information we can more rationally decide what to do with their comments.

Resilient people use information, facts and evidence to make their case. Rather than react defensively, they weigh-up what they know and respond accordingly.

MEANING, PURPOSE & WELLBEING

FIND MEANING IN THE MOMENTS

On occasion, take time to consider even
the simplest of things…

The skittering of a squirrel,
The bee collecting nectar,
The clouds that gather in the sky…

Contemplate a happy meaning behind
the things you experience.
Get into the habit of seeking
a positive frame…

*Resilience can mean making choices as to
how we make meaning about the world
around us. Every situation, no matter how
challenging, can offer you a gift.*

MAKE MEANING... PURPOSEFULLY!

When things happen in life, how we interpret them affects how we feel.

For example, if someone you know appears to 'blank you' when they pass you by, check in with yourself:
"What does that mean to me?"

If your interpretation leads to you feeling bad in some way, ask yourself:
"What else could it mean?"

We are meaning makers.
Each event has only the meaning we give it.
If the meaning we make leads us to be
unhappy, we can seek
alternative meanings!

WHAT IS THE POINT?

Some people ask this question in despair and disillusionment.

However, the trick is to find (or create) an answer.
Indeed, an answer is required!

"What's the point?" is an invitation to plug back in to your sense of purpose!

People with a sense of purpose, who can then 'plug back in' through tough times… these are the people who bounce back… these are the people with resilient focus!

CHOOSE YOUR PURPOSE

Aside from 'who am I?',
the biggest question you can ask
yourself is 'why am I here?'…
What are you here for?
What are you here to learn, to give,
to contribute?

The trick is not necessarily to discover
these things (although that can be fun),
but to CHOOSE them.

*Resilience is easier when you have a strong
sense of who you are, what you are here for
and hence what is truly important to you.*

THE PURPOSE OF LIFE?

Perhaps there is no universal 'answer'
or purpose of life…

Unless 'The Purpose of Life'
is to create your own personal purpose
of life, and then living it to the full!

Stop seeking The Purpose and
make up <u>your</u> purpose!
And if it isn't fulfilling you,
change it!

*People with strong self-esteem appear to
have their own guiding principles,
and they have the confidence to update
those that are not working!*

CONTRIBUTE

What can you do to help others?

Write a list of things you could happily do that might make someone else's life just that little bit better.

Join others in doing good things for good causes…
Or do something simple that others may not even notice
(like pick up a piece of litter)…
Or consider some
'acts of random kindness'.

When we contribute to the greater good (without the desire for reward or acknowledgement), it can bring an extraordinary sense of wellbeing!

WE ARE STARDUST...

Did you know that we were all once
the centre of a star!
Most of the elements that make up our
bodies were forged in the heat of a star.

We are all made of the same.
No-one else is more valuable than you.

*People with strong self-esteem
value themselves **and** they value others.
They accept that no-one is better than
them... and they are not better than others.*

DESIGNER YOU

How do you want to be known and remembered by others?

List three qualities that you would love to be known for…

Now consider how you might live and breath these qualities. What behaviours would mean that people remembered you the way you'd like to be remembered?
How would you treat others and how would you treat yourself?

The most confident and 'self-actualised' people are amazingly consistent in the way they interact with other people and the world in general.

A PURPOSE STATEMENT!

If you had a motto or life-mantra,
what would it be?

Do you have a purpose statement,
a guiding beacon of light,
an internal compass heading,
a due North?

Start with the phrase:
"I do what I do in order to…" or
"In everything I do, I seek to …"

Without a purpose statement, how will
you know you are on track?

A sense of purpose can give us criteria for living life to the fullest and the 'fulfillest'!

IMPOSTROUS!

At some point in their life,
most people have experienced
'Imposter Syndrome'.
This is the feeling that we don't belong
in such an 'elite' group or deserve to be
at the level we have reached.

Look around the room and
know that others may be
questioning themselves too!
They might even be looking at you and
thinking how confident you seem!

You do belong.
You have every right to be here.

*Resilience means building your self-esteem,
allowing that you are on a journey and that
your experience will develop over time.*

FOCUS ON 'IMPORTANT' (1)

Take time to write a list of the people and things that are particularly important to you in your life.

Make sure you spend time with those people that matter to you
(or at least send them a message from time to time).

In your list, make sure you remember some of the things associated with your wellbeing and health.

Resilient people know what is important to them… they make these things a priority and give them full attention.

FOCUS ON 'IMPORTANT' (2)

Happiness is focusing on those things that matter to you in your life.

During tough times, or times of change, remind yourself of the things that matter. Bring them to mind and focus on them.

The happiest people are those that purposefully focus their attention and memory to the things that truly matter in their life

HOW IMPORTANT IS THAT ISSUE?

When life throws something unexpected at you, ask yourself: "How important is this really?"

So often we get caught in the drama of a situation that, on reflection, had very little impact on our life.

People with strong self-esteem are able to gauge what really matters in their life. They are then able to see the 'dramas' as just fleeting moments of hassle.

POSITIVE FOCAL POINTS

Take time to create and identify a list of 'positive focal points'.
These are the things that make you feel good when you think about them.

What are the things you enjoy doing?
What do you look forward to?
Organise and do the things you enjoy!

Who are the people (and/or pets) you love being with?
Spend time with them!

When times get tough, resilient people have a list of 'positive focal points' that they can think about to remind themselves of the good things in life.

LET GO OF THE PAINFUL

Let go of blame.
Learn and move on.

Let go of guilt.
Learn and move on.

Learn not to repeat the things that hurt.
Then forgive yourself
and forgive others.

*Resilient people aim to improve themselves
and to do no harm. They also understand
that to say or do the 'wrong thing' is part of
being human.
For that reason, they learn, forgive and
move on.*

LET GO OF BEING RIGHT!

Too many people fight to be Right,
as if they know the Truth!

Let go of being right and
needing to be right.
Let go of thinking
that you have the truth.

No-one holds the objective truth,
and it would be pure arrogance to
think we did!
All we have is our own personal
opinion and belief.

*The strongest minded people are those that
can allow for other 'rights' and other
'truths' in the world.
The weakest minds are those without
flexibility.*

THERE COMES A TIME IN LIFE

When you reflect back on your life, do
you think: "I wish I'd…"
or "I'm glad I…"?
If you have a bit of both,
which list is longer?

And what could you do or begin today
that one day you will be looking back
and thinking: "I'm glad I…"?

*The most fulfilled people understand
that today is the day to begin
to make those things happen…
that one day you'll be looking back and
thinking you were glad you did!*

MAKE A RESOURCE POT!

Create a 'resource pot' by writing down a list of your positive traits, memories, characteristics, qualities, motivators and achievements.

What do you enjoy doing?
What gives you a buzz?
What moves you?
What is important to you?
What do you love?
What are you proud of?
Where have you made a difference?

Resilient people develop and utilise as many resources as they can find! The more the resources… the greater the resilience!

LOOKING FORWARD TO?

Create things in your life that you can genuinely look forward to.

Of course, it is important to 'be in the present moment', but that doesn't stop us from organising wonderful future 'present moments'!

Do things you like doing and also do something different! Go places you like going and also go somewhere different!

To be resilient is to have resources that we can feel good about.
The future can be a delightful resource of potential and possibilities.

UNDERSTAND YOUR VALUES

For every theme and context in life,
you will have a set of values associated.

For example, consider the following
themes one by one:
Relationships,
Family,
Work/Career,
Home.

And for each theme, ask yourself:
"What is important to me about…"
Push yourself to come up with at least
seven things for each theme.

*When you understand your values, you can
make decisions and take actions
accordingly.*

UNDERSTAND YOUR NEEDS

In any situation you find yourself,
you can ask yourself:
"What specifically do I need here?"

If other people are involved,
ask yourself:
"And what might they need?"
(And if you don't know,
consider asking!)

By knowing what you need (and others too), it is easier to be assertive.

THE GOOD OLD DAYS

Do you remember the past
with 'rose tinted glasses'?
Do you think back on certain events
with fondness?
Does nostalgia play a part in your life?
Do you have others that you share
memories with?
Have you ever been
wonderfully wistful?

*Positive reminiscing is recommended
within the field of Positive Psychology.
Happy people remember and
share happy memories!*

IT'S OKAY TO TAKE 'ME' TIME!

Personal time is important,
perhaps to recharge your batteries.

When do you get the time to simply be
'you'… without having to fulfil a role
(e.g. parent, colleague, manager)?

Seek out some time during the week
for reflection and meditation… maybe
take a bath with the door closed!

*Resilient people endeavour to be there for
other people but they also take time
on their own… just to be!*

IT'S OKAY TO TREAT YOURSELF!

Reward yourself from time to time
(whilst staying within your means)!

Do something nice for yourself.
Buy yourself a little something
(and then make use of it).

Resilient people are prepared to reward themselves from time to time… but they also understand the boundaries of finances and the consequences of unhealthy compulsions!

IT'S OKAY TO LOOK AFTER YOURSELF

Eat healthily and exercise,
go for walks in nature,
take time to relax,
spend time with friends and family,
look after your appearance…

Simple as that!

People with stronger self-esteem tend to look after their bodies and their appearance, partly for health reasons and partly to feel good about looking good!

CHANGE HOW YOU FEEL

CHANGE HOW YOU FEEL

EMOTIONS ARE NATURAL!

Some people seem to beat themselves up for having emotions or 'being emotional'.

However, emotional reactions to situations are natural!

Notice your emotions.
If each emotion has a message for you, what might it be communicating?

Emotions are physiological, 'brain chemistry' responses to the environment. People with strong emotional intelligence learn to identify emotions and what the emotions may be 'trying to tell them'.

EMOTIONS ARE NOT BAD... EVEN THE 'BAD' ONES!

There are some emotions that tend to get labelled as 'negative'.
However, all emotions serve a purpose.

It is not the emotion itself that is problematic, it is what we <u>do</u> with the emotion, i.e. how we express it or behave when we feel a certain way.

Emotional intelligence informs us that even the so called 'bad' emotions help us to live and survive. For example:
Anger can be the fire for change.
Sadness tells us that something important to us is missing.
Fear encourages us to be wary and to prepare for what may come.
Embarrassment can be a message not to repeat a behaviour.

EMPATHY vs SYMPATHY

Some folk seem to wear
other people's pain like a cloak…
this is Sympathy.

When dealing with other people who
are upset and/or in tears,
be there for them…
a shoulder to cry on perhaps.

But remember that their hurt is
<u>their</u> hurt and not yours.

If you want to help them,
empathise… feel <u>for</u> them,
but don't try to take on their hurt.

*When someone is in a hole,
don't get in the hole with them…
offer them a ladder instead!*

EMOTIONS ARE PROCESSES

It can be helpful to stop treating emotions as 'things', particularly if we feel emotionally stuck.

Whilst we talk about 'having emotions' as if they are possessions, they are really processes we 'go through'.
To go through an emotion is a healthier way of experiencing it…
We move through an emotion… and out the other side!

If you are feeling less than happy, try asking yourself:
"As I move through this emotion, I wonder what the next feeling will be?"

Emotions are active, moving experiences…
the clue is in the word e-motion!

EMOTIONS AND MOODS

Consider that moods sit in the background to emotions.
Moods last for hours (or days) and emotions usually last for minutes.
A mood will tend to influence the emotions we feel.

Rather than talking about being 'in' a mood, try changing that to 'doing' a mood?
For example, if you feel irritable, notice what it feels like to say:
"I am doing irritable at the moment!"

This can help to put you in the driving seat of your moods.

The way we think and talk about a mood can affect how we experience it.

HOW DO YOU WANT TO FEEL?

Focus on how you want to feel,
rather than how you don't want to feel.

Instead of saying "I don't want to feel stressed", focus on the feeling you want, e.g. "I want to feel calm/happy/confident/excited".

Write a list of feelings, emotions and states that you would like to experience more of… more often.

*Positive states are resources.
Resilient people are resourceful…
They have a long list of favourite feelings
that they can focus on!*

EMOTIONS WANT TO BE EXPRESSED

The outcome of an emotion is to be expressed, so that it leaves our body instead of festering.

If you sometimes struggle to identify your emotions at the time, try the following 'ALE' model:
Acknowledge (I feel something!)
Label (I am feeling 'X')
Express (Say/write down how you feel)

(An emotion doesn't necessarily need to be expressed 'at' the person we believe caused it!)

Resilient people understand that emotions flow through us and then need to be released.

SEEK STILLNESS

To help 'centre' yourself,
sit in a quiet place.
Then notice any 'noise' in your mind.

To any internal chatter
or stray thoughts,
say gently but firmly (in your mind):
"Stop!"

The aim to is sit with a 'quiet mind',
free of noise.

*Resilience means taking control of your
inner world and your internal dialogue.
The word 'noise' has connections with both
'nausea' and 'noxious'…
so take time to detox your mind!*

FIND YOUR OWN MOTIVATION MOTTO

It may seem 'cheesy' or silly, but find
(or write) your own motivation mantra.
For example, you might use
the ancient Roman phrase:
"Fortune Favours the Brave".
Want more success in your life?
Be brave and take steps to
make it happen!

*Resilient people have phrases they use to
pick themselves up and get moving again.*

GET A THEME TUNE!

What music or song lifts you, moves you forward or gets you 'rocking'? Alternatively, what music relaxes you and helps you to chill out?
Play the music in your head… or sing it to yourself… and then you'll always have your own theme tune!

Music can change the way we feel…
in an instant.

HANDLING NEGATIVE EXPERIENCES

If you have an experience that leaves
you feeling unhappy,
Write down what happened
and how you felt.
This can help you gain distance
from the negative memory.

(This can also help with preventing
recurring nightmares.)

*Research in positive psychology suggests
that journaling can help reduce the
negative emotions associated with
an experience.*

HANDLE THE NEGATIVE THOUGHTS

Some people are mean to themselves! Perhaps their internal dialogue has become negative or they are limiting or belittling themselves in some way.

If you ever do this to yourself, imagine a person standing next to you saying those mean things to you… what would you say to them? "Back off!" or "Stop it!" perhaps?

Do the same with destructive thoughts. Tell that thought (kindly but assertively) to stop it.

Some folks are their own worst enemy. However, resilient people find ways to shut down those destructive parts.

KNOW THY BUTTONS!

The Oracle at Delphi carried the message: "Know Thyself".
Here we are suggesting you get to know your 'buttons'!

What are some of the things that trigger an emotional reaction in you? What behaviours in others make you automatically (*and perhaps irrationally*) angry, upset or afraid?

By knowing your buttons, you can more easily control your reactions.

Resilient people don't necessarily seek to become button-free (AKA Enlightened!) but instead understand the kinds of behaviours that trigger their emotions. When they notice a 'button-push', they can more easily step back and become more objective.

DISSOLVE YOUR ANGER

If you find yourself getting angry with someone, seek to empathise with them in some way.

Remember that we can all be difficult sometimes… ask yourself:
"Under what circumstances might I behave like that?"

Alternatively consider that
a difficult person is a person in difficulty.
You are more likely to want to help a person in difficulty... ask yourself:
"What must they have gone through to make them behave like that?"

Empathy dissolves anger!

WHY WORRY!

If you find yourself worrying about a situation or event, find ways to reassure yourself.

Imagine you are talking to a small child who is scared… what would you say to them to calm and strengthen them?

Imagine that the worried part of you is like that child.
Talk to that part of you inside to lovingly reassure yourself.

Resilient people understand that fear is driven by just a part of themselves.
They can then take responsibility for that part instead of letting it run them.

HANDLING THE AFTER-EFFECTS

If we experience a difficult event,
we may well come out the other side
feeling less than positive.

Sometimes that feeling is shock.

Remember, shock is a natural response
to an unexpected situation.
You may need a little time to get
through that before you can
bounce back.

*When we experience shock,
we do need time to recover.
The more resilient we are,
the easier and quicker the recovery.*

DON'T GET JEALOUS… GET INSPIRED!

If you see that someone else has something you want…
figure out how they got it and get inspired to find your own way of achieving something similar.

Resilience is about admiring other people for their successes and where appropriate, learning from them!

BE HAPPY NOW!

Have you ever heard someone say:
"I'll be happy when…"
(for example: "I'll be happy when
I win the lottery!")

Whilst this may seem an innocent statement, it can create a problem… When people make their happiness reliant on external events, they are no longer in the driving seat.

So… be happy for no reason at all!

Building resilience means owning your emotions and not making how you feel reliant on external factors.

FORWARD WIND

If you find yourself feeling less than positive about an event that is coming up in the near future, try the 'Forward Wind Technique'!

In your mind, project yourself beyond the future event to a time when you will be feeling good again.

For example, if someone is feeling nervous about doing a presentation tomorrow, they can 'forward wind' to tomorrow night where they can feel relieved and relaxed!

Resilient people tend to focus on the feelings they want... i.e. those that make them feel more resourceful.

ABOUT THE AUTHORS

ABOUT THE AUTHORS

Joe and Melody Cheal have been involved in the Personal & Professional Development fields since 1993, gathering best practise from all walks of life and business. They have personally trained and coached over 20,000 people, helping them revolutionise the way they interact and work with others.

They have been married since 1994 and continue to help each other stay happily resilient!

Joe Cheal

Joe is the Lead Imaginarian and Trainer for Imaginarium Learning & Development. He has been involved in the field of management and organisational development since 1993.
In focusing his training, coaching and consultancy experience within the business environment, he has worked with a broad range of organisational sectors and cultures, helping thousands of people revolutionise the way they work with others.

He holds an MSc in Organisational Development and Neuro Linguistic Technologies (his MSc dissertation was an exploration into 'social paradox'), a degree in Philosophy and Psychology and diplomas in Coaching and Psychotherapy.

Joe is an NLP Master Trainer who enjoys learning new things... by exploring diverse fields of science, philosophy and psychology and then integrating these 'learnings'. He is the author of *'Solving Impossible Problems', 'Who Stole My Pie?'* and the co-author of *'The Model Presenter'* and *'The Relationship Dance'*. He is also the editor of *Powered by NLP 1 & 2* and the journal *Acuity*.

He is a volunteer mentor for the University of Sussex Business School and an active committee member and regular speaker for the CIPD.

Melody Cheal

Melody lives on the edge of Ashdown Forest, East Sussex with her husband, Joe and two dogs. She has a degree in Psychology, an MSc in Applied Positive Psychology, a diploma in Psychotherapy and is an NLP Master Practitioner and Certified NLP Master Trainer. She is a qualified Hypnotherapist and Hypnosis Trainer.

She is part of the external verification panel for the ANLP accreditation programme. Her Psychological Approaches to Coaching Diploma is accredited by the Association for Coaching.

She regularly speaks at national conferences and has presented her dissertation research, 'NLP and self-esteem', at an international research conference. Her work was published in an academic journal as a result. She is the author of *'Becoming Happy'* and the co-author of the popular books, *'The Model Presenter'* and *'The Relationship Dance'*.

Imaginarium
LEARNING & DEVELOPMENT

Imaginarium Learning & Development is a consultancy that specialises in inspiring the natural potential of organisations, leadership, management and individuals through OD, L&D and Executive Coaching.

We work with clients from a broad range of sectors and aim to work in partnership with our clients, enhancing the profile of leadership, learning and development in our client's organisation.

Since 1993 we have experience of working with thousands of people from many organisations including:

Adoption UK, Aeroflex, Amnesty International, ARA (Aircraft Research Association), Association of Local Councils, Astra Zeneca & AstraTech, Autoglass, Avondale, Balfour Beatty, Bedford Borough Council, Beds Health, Beds Magistrates Courts Committee, Belron, Berry Gardens, Bio-Products Laboratories (BPL), Birdlife and Plantlife, British Broadcasting Company (BBC), British Gas, BT, Calderdale Council, Cambridge City Council, Cambridge University Libraries, Cambridge University Press, Camelot, Canon UK & Europe, Care UK, Cellnet, Central Bedfordshire, Church Conservation Trust, Cognita Schools, Cranfield University, Dixons Stores Group International, Emmaus Village Carlton, GSK, Herts County Council, Herts Magistrates

Courts Committee, Hertsmere Borough Council, Inland Revenue, Institute of Engineering & Technology (IET), J. Murphy & Sons, Langley Search & Selection, Legal & General, Lockheed Martin, London Borough of Camden, Luton Borough Council, MCA, Mercedes AMG High Performance Powertrains Ltd, Mylan Pharma, Newham Council, NHS, North Herts District Council, OAG, Olympic Blinds, RSPB, Sainsbury's, Santander, Serco, Shepherd Stubbs Recruitment, Staverton Park Conference Centre, Teignbridge District Council, Tesco, The Assessment Network, Three Rivers District Council, TOPRA, Tunbridge Wells Borough Council, University of Hertfordshire, University of Kent, University of Sussex, Welwyn Hatfield Borough Council, Welwyn Hatfield Community Housing Trust, Willmott Dixon, The Wine Society.

Imaginarium offers a range of consultancy services including:
- Training courses
- Executive coaching and skills coaching
- Facilitation and team development
- Change management, Organisational development and Learning & Development consultancy
- Strategic engineering and Paradox management
- Myers Briggs profiling and Emotional Intelligence testing

Why work with Imaginarium?

Here are 4 things that make us special…

Experience
Imagine tapping into a wellspring of experience to help your people become more effective, more efficient and even more resourceful.

We have been involved in the learning & development environment for a quarter of a century! In the training and coaching environment, we have encountered and understood the majority of problems and challenges that human beings can face. We are able to draw from a wealth of practical resources, solutions, examples, models, hints, tips and ideas to help get people unstuck (and to help them 'unstick' themselves!) As individuals, we continue to learn and develop, keeping what we do fresh and engaging. We 'get' people!

Credibility
Imagine working with a company who regard your success and credibility as highly as their own.

We value not only our own credibility but also the credibility of the company we work with. We know that when we are training and coaching in your company, we represent "learning & development". We are passionate about advancing the reputation and culture of people development in organisations. We have worked with a vast range of organisational sectors and cultures giving us the ability to adapt from one company to another. We have also worked with some highly multicultural organisations, from people from all across the globe.

Humour & Enjoyment

Imagine your staff… keen to develop themselves to become even better at what they do.

We love what we do! People who train with us enjoy themselves. We've been told that some people laugh and smile more in one day than they normally do in a week! We believe that enjoyment and light-heartedness are one of the most important keys to learning. Wherever we have embedded into an organisation's culture, people want to attend courses!

Return on Investment

Imagine working with people who care that their service adds measurable value.

It is important to us that whatever we do, it adds value for your company. Sometimes this can be realised in terms of financial profits and savings. Sometimes return on investment is subtler in terms of staff motivation, efficiency and improved communication. Whether the returns are tangible or intangible we are keen to make sure that we are worth our weight in gold!

Our courses and topics include:

LEADERSHIP DEVELOPMENT
Change Management
Coaching Performance
Delegate!
Feedback for Effectiveness
Making Meetings Work
Management Development Programmes
Managing People Successfully
Mentor Skills
Motivate!
Project Leadership
Team Building and Development

RESULTS AND RELATIONSHIPS
Assertiveness: Clarity and Focus
Building Partnerships
Communication
Conflict Resolution
Customer Care
Dealing with Aggression
Dealing with Difficult People
Handling Conflict in Meetings
Influence and Persuasion
Magic of Mediation
Negotiation Skills
Understanding Personalities

IN FRONT OF THE AUDIENCE
Advanced Presentation Skills
The Essential Presenter
Persuasive Presentations
Train the Trainer

PERSONAL IMPACT
Career & Profile Development
Coping with Change
Dealing With Pressure
Innovation: Getting Creative
Managing Your Performance
Resilience: Developing the 'Bounce Back' Factor
Time Management
Understanding & Managing Unconscious Bias
Wellbeing: Staying Psychologically Healthy
Who Stole My Pie?

EXECUTIVE DEVELOPMENT
Advanced Negotiation Skills
Becoming a Mentor
Beyond Selling
Making NLP Work
Managing Tensions
Organisational Development
Organisational Politics
Storytelling in Business
Strategic Change Management
Troubleshooting: Problem Resolution
Working with Transactional Analysis

HR SKILLS FOR MANAGERS
Appraisal
Capability & Disciplinary
Controlling Absence
Dealing with Poor Performance
Introduction to Counselling
Managing Difficult People
Recruitment Selection & Interviewing
Tackling Bullying & Harassment

Psychological Approaches to Coaching - Diploma

Accredited by the Association for Coaching

The programme is designed to allow learners time to reflect, consolidate and practice between modules. Each module is three days in length and includes supervised coaching practice with feedback.

For experienced coaches there is the opportunity to dip into the programme and attend individual modules. As this course is accredited by the Association for Coaches the modules can be used as CPD.

The modules are:
- Foundations in Coaching
- Transactional Analysis for Coaches
- Using the iNLP Coaching frame work
- Positive Psychology Coaching

GWizNLP

Training in Neuro-linguistic Programming (NLP)

NLP (Neuro-linguistic Programming) could be described as the psychology of excellence and the science of change. Through understanding more about how the mind/brain works (neuro) and how language affects us (linguistic), a practitioner is able to initiate and sustain change (programming) on a personal, interpersonal and organisational level.

NLP was designed originally to model excellence. By establishing exactly how someone achieves something, excellence can be modelled, taught to someone else and repeated again and again. From this starting point, over the last thirty years, an array of processes, concepts and techniques have been developed to enable you to:

- become more resourceful in managing attitudes, thoughts, emotions, behaviours and beliefs
- relate to others easily and effortlessly,
- understand how language and its use has a direct impact on your state, your brain and your success in communicating with others.

In addition to all this, as a GWiz NLP practitioner, you will learn techniques designed to help you develop your own skills and help others develop theirs. The principles will be introduced conversationally and with activities throughout the course allowing you to learn on many levels consciously and unconsciously.

As NLP Master Trainers we offer the complete three levels of certified NLP courses throughout the year:

- NLP 101
- NLP Diploma
- NLP Practitioner
- NLP Master Practitioner
- NLP Trainer's Training

We also offer Accredited Hypnotherapist training from entry level through to Hypnosis Trainer.

As part of the ongoing support offered to all our students Melody provides supervision groups, mentoring and personal support to our graduates. This support is available to practitioners trained elsewhere.

If you are interested in personal and professional development and would like to more about NLP, have a look at our website: www.gwiznlp.com or contact us: info@gwiznlp.com.

Other Books from GWiz Publishing

Becoming Happy!
Lessons from Nature

By Melody Cheal

The search for happiness can often seem elusive and so this book provides hope for those wanting help in becoming happy.

Find out how to unlock the best version of you, recognising your own sense of worth and value. Melody shares experiences from her own journey of self-discovery plus tools and ideas she uses in her own practice.

The combination of pictures drawn from nature plus simple easy to apply exercises provides the reader with tools to begin transformation.

Are you ready to Be Brilliant?

Other Books from GWiz Publishing

WHO STOLE MY PIE?

By Joe Cheal

How to manage priorities, boundaries and expectations

Walter's lunch... and his time are being eaten into.

Fortunately, 'real-world' help is at hand to help him manage his time... and inadvertently, his pies!

Join Walter in learning how to manage priorities, boundaries and expectations...

Make your life easier and more fulfilling!

Who Stole My Pie is packed with powerfully simple models, tools, tips and techniques. If you want to gain greater control over your time then this book is for you!

Other Books from GWiz Publishing

The Relationship Dance

How would your life be, if you and your partner were <u>always</u> on the same side... facing life's challenges <u>together</u>?

A relationship is a dynamic pattern of advancing and retreating 'energies'. A *healthy* relationship is a graceful dance of balanced and constructive interactions. Indeed, the quality of your life is determined by the health of your relationships.

The Relationship Dance is a guide for anyone who wants to improve their ability to relate, communicate and share happiness and meaning with a loved one!

In this book, you will discover how to:
- Create a solid foundation with the *Five Relationship Graces*
- Remain *balanced* and *constructive*, even when you face differences
- 'Clean up your own act' to develop a healthy and rewarding relationship
- Build and maintain a *complementary* and *interdependent* relationship
- Communicate assertively and *speak your truth with kindness*
- Revivify that 'honeymoon feeling'

Other Books from GWiz Publishing

THE LITTLE BOOK OF PERSUASION
UPDATED

If you were more persuasive...

What would your life be like?
Where might you be and what might you have?
Where could you go and what could you achieve?

The Little Book of Persuasion is bursting
with practical idea for using anywhere.
Build relationships and get better results
at home, at work
and out in the big wide world!

Other Books from GWiz Publishing

the
MODEL
presenter

By Joe & Melody Cheal

The Model Presenter will show you how to:
- Develop the qualities of an exceptional presenter
- Create a memorable and logical structure
- Deliver presentations and training with confidence
- Engage an audience easily and effortlessly
- Deal with a wide range of challenging situations

This 'how-to' guide is filled with steps to follow and helpful hints and tips modelled on the best of the best.

You will discover a host of original material including:
* Closing the Gap between yourself and the Mind of the Audience
* Preparing using the BROADCAST Model
* Delivering training sessions using the IMPACT Formula
* Transforming nerves into confidence

Be remembered for the right reasons...
As you become **the Model Presenter***!*

Other Books from GWiz Publishing

SOLVING IMPOSSIBLE PROBLEMS

By Joe Cheal

*Say goodbye to organisational dilemmas, tensions, conflicts and stress with **Solving Impossible Problems**.*

The ability to manage tensions, paradox and uncertainty in business is becoming a much sought-after leadership skill.
'Paradox Management' is a new but increasingly essential field in the area of business management and will be highly influential in the ongoing sanity and success of all organisations and of the people who work for them.

Solving Impossible Problems will give you a greater understanding of organisational tensions and paradox. You will learn how to recognise these 'twisty turny' problems and then use practical tools to resolve them or use them for innovation.

*This book is a unique guide to heightened wellbeing and enhanced thinking power through the revolutionary process of **Paradox Management**.*

For more information about
Joe & Melody Cheal,
Imaginarium Learning & Development
and/or GWiz NLP,
you can contact us at:

E: info@imaginariumdev.com
E: info@gwiznlp.com

Ph: 01892 309205

W: www.imaginariumdev.com
W: www.gwizNLP.com

Lightning Source UK Ltd.
Milton Keynes UK
UKHW012022020519
341997UK00006B/529/P